KEVIN JOHNSON

THRIVE

DARE TO LIVE LIKE JESUS

HIGHER
SERIES

ZONDERVAN®

ZONDERVAN.com/
AUTHORTRACKER
follow your favorite authors

**youth
specialties**

YOUTH SPECIALTIES

Thrive: Dare to Live Like Jesus
Copyright 2009 by Kevin Johnson

Youth Specialties resources, 300 S. Pierce St., El Cajon, CA 92020 are published by Zondervan, 5300 Patterson Ave. SE, Grand Rapids, MI 49530.

ISBN 978-0-310-28265-5

Cover design by David Conn
Interior design by SharpSeven Design

Printed in the United States of America

09 10 11 12 13 14 • 20 19 18 17 16 15 14 13 12 11 10 9 8 7 6 5 4 3 2 1

Contents

Start Here

It's time to let your faith fly HIGHER. If you're ready to take your relationship with God to the next level, this series of books shows you how.

Thrive contains 20 Bible studies that lead you upward. You'll find Scriptures that speak to the core of your life, along with space to express what's on your mind. You'll think for yourself and discover significant insights you might not find on your own. *Thrive* shows you how to break free and be different from the rest of the world. You'll find out how to live the thoroughly transformed life God wants you to enjoy. And you'll figure out for yourself why you don't want to settle for anything less.

Don't rush through *Thrive*. You can do a study per day, a study per week, or anything between. Actually, the slower you go, the more you'll gain. Each study is just a few pages long but provides you plenty to think about and act on. The end of each study comes with added material to let you fly even higher.

You'll see that every study opens with a mostly-blank page that has a single Bible verse that sums up the main point. These verses are worth memorizing, as a way to fill your head with the amazing truths of God's Word. Then comes **START**, a brief introduction to get you into the topic. **READ** takes you to a Scripture passage. You can read the verses here in the book or, if you want, grab your own Bible and read the passage there. **THINK** helps you examine the main ideas of the text, and **LIVE** makes it easy to apply what you learn. **WRAP** pulls everything together.

Then there's some bonus material. **MORE THOUGHTS TO MULL** tosses you a few more questions to ask yourself or others. **MORE SCRIPTURES TO DIG** leads you to related Bible passages to help you hear even more from God on the topic.

Whether you read on your own or get together with a group, *Thrive* will help your faith fly high. It's your chance to grab the best that God has in store for you.

Kevin Johnson

1. LIVE IT UP

Romans 12:1 (NCV)

So brothers and sisters, since God has shown us great mercy, I beg you to offer your lives as a living sacrifice to him. Your offering must be only for God and pleasing to him, which is the spiritual way for you to worship.

START Living for God might sound risky—until you realize everything he's done for you. Giving him your all might feel like the losing end of a bargain—until you're amazed by his moment-by-moment care for you. God overflows with kindness, fairness, and intelligence. His plans for you are the best path you could ever pick. And his Son died to give you life. Whether or not you fully experience God's greatness, however, is up to you. It all starts when you open yourself up to him.

Why would you want to live it up—give your whole life to God? Why wouldn't you?

READ Romans 12:1-2 (NCV)

> [1] So brothers and sisters, since God has shown us great mercy, I beg you to offer your lives as a living sacrifice to him. Your offering must be only for God and pleasing to him, which is the spiritual way for you to worship. [2] Do not be shaped by this world; instead be changed within by a new way of thinking. Then you will be able to decide what God wants for you; you will know what is good and pleasing to him and what is perfect.

THINK The phrase "since God has shown us great mercy" points back to everything God has done for us—acts that are spelled out in the first 11 chapters of Romans. The short version: Even though people consistently do wrong, God has rebuilt our relationship with him through the death and rising again of Jesus. And through the Holy Spirit, he is present with us right now to make us into new people.

Say it in your own words: How has God shown us "great mercy" and compassion?

Because God has been so kind to us, we should offer ourselves to him as a "living sacrifice." What's that?

You might assume you have to live for God to get his love. The Bible says it works just the opposite. God lavishes you with his love so you'll want to give yourself back to him.

What happens when you allow God to change the way you think?

LIVE Why is it "worship" when you give yourself totally to God?

What parts of your life do you let God rule? In what areas do you tend to do your own thing?

What is your biggest struggle? Where do you most need God's help?

WRAP God doesn't just urge you to be a living sacrifice. He tells you how. When you let God fill your mind with the real facts of life—about you, him, and his plan for you to thrive in your everyday world—you'll grasp what he wants you to do and you'll desire to do it to your utmost. When you allow God to remake you, you change from the inside out. It becomes natural to commit your whole life to him.

» MORE THOUGHTS TO MULL

- Start a list of all the things God has done (and continues to do) for you. Put the list where you will see it often. How does looking at that list impact your attitude toward God?

- What does it mean that "the world" shapes how you think? List some examples and explain.

- Romans 12:1, in the majestic King James Version of the Bible, says that offering yourself to God is "your reasonable service." What's reasonable about living for God? What seems like it's not reasonable?

» MORE SCRIPTURES TO DIG

- Have no doubts: God wants to help you thrive. Like Jesus said in **John 10:10**, "I have come that they may have life, and have it to the full." Read **Jeremiah 29:11** to discover God's unbeatable plans for you.

- Despite our worst mistakes and failings, we never have to beg God to love us. He loves us even when we don't love him back. Get it straight from **Romans 5:8**: "But God demonstrates his own love for us in this: While we were still sinners, Christ died for us."

- The method God uses to train you to think differently isn't a mystery. He reshapes your thinking as you absorb Scripture and everything it teaches. Read **Psalm 19:7-14** and **2 Timothy 3:16-17** for details on exactly what the Bible does for you. The more of God's Word you take in, the more readily you will offer yourself to him.

- God knows you better than anyone else does. And he values you as his one-of-a-kind creation. Read **Psalm 139:1-16** to get a God's-eye view of you.

2. GET IT RIGHT

You are accepted by God in Jesus

Romans 3:25 (NLT)

People are made right with God when they believe that Jesus sacrificed his life, shedding his blood.

START If God were Santa Claus, we'd all show up on his naughty list. Actually, "naughty" is way too kind a word for how human beings act when they are separated from God. We're all sinners—people who have run far from the One who loves us most. Romans 3:11-12 says, "No one is truly wise; no one is seeking God. All have turned away from God; all have become useless. No one does good, not a single one" (NLT). No matter how hard we try to keep God's rules for living and relating to him, we fail. We've shattered our relationship with him. But he devised a way to bring us back to himself.

Suppose God rattled off every sin you've ever committed, then asked you why he should be your friend. What would you say?

READ Romans 3:22-26 (NLT)

> 22 We are made right with God by placing our faith in Jesus Christ. And this is true for everyone who believes, no matter who we are. 23 For everyone has sinned; we all fall short of God's glorious standard. 24 Yet God, with undeserved kindness, declares that we are righteous. He did this through Christ Jesus when he freed us from the penalty for our sins. 25 For God presented Jesus as the sacrifice for sin. People are made right with God when they believe that Jesus sacrificed his life, shedding his blood. This sacrifice shows that God was being fair when he held back and did not punish those who sinned in times past, 26 for he was looking ahead and including them in what he would do in this present time. God did this to demonstrate his righteousness, for he himself is fair and just, and he declares sinners to be right in his sight when they believe in Jesus.

THINK What standard have all people missed?

Even good people don't come anywhere close to God's perfection. So who does God declare "right in his sight"? Why does he do that?

God says that the punishment for sin is death, but Jesus paid that ultimate penalty for you when he died on the cross (Romans 6:23). When God makes you right with himself—an action called "justification" in many versions of the Bible—he declares you righteous, not guilty of sin. Justification means it's "just as if" you've never sinned. There's nothing you can do to earn this spotlessly clean record. His forgiveness is a free gift, motivated by kindness you don't deserve. You are justified by faith in Jesus—made right with God through believing Jesus died for you.

Who can take advantage of God's offer to get right with him through Jesus?

LIVE Say it in your words: How do you get right with God?

These verses from Romans wrap together some basic truths: You've sinned. Whatever good things you might do aren't enough to earn God's approval. But when you admit your sins to God and trust that Jesus died on your behalf, you become friends with God. That's what being made right through faith is all about. It's the only way you're accepted by him.

Does Jesus dying for the wrong things we've done seem like a good way for God to deal with sin? Why—or why not?

Agree or disagree—and explain your answer: Trusting in the death of Jesus for our sins is the only way human beings get right with God.

WRAP As good as some people look on the outside, none of us match God's perfection. Compared to him we all fall short. We can never become acceptable to God based on what we do. We gain a real relationship with God only through faith in Jesus.

»   MORE THOUGHTS TO MULL

- Why has God "held back" from giving human beings the punishment we deserve?

- Make a list of all the things you've done that you think make you look good to God. Then tear it up—and say thanks to God for sending Jesus to make you right with him.

- If you've never told God that you trust Christ's death on your behalf, tell him now—and tell a mature Christian about your decision.

» MORE SCRIPTURES TO DIG

- God's love is beyond amazing. "He does not treat us as our sins deserve," **Psalm 103:10** says, "or repay us according to our iniquities."

- Read **Colossians 1:21-23** for another tight summary of how we become friends with God through Jesus.

- Look at **Galatians 3:1-25** to see how the apostle Paul chews out people trying to get right with God by good deeds.

- Check out everything God gives you when you become his friend: Not only does he declare you "not guilty" of sin (**Romans 3:24**), but you also get peace with him (**Romans 5:1**). You've been adopted by a loving parent who will never abandon you (**Galatians 3:26**). God rejoices over you (**Zephaniah 3:17**). You can boldly run into God's presence (**Hebrews 10:19-22**).

3. PRICELESS

You are insanely valuable

1 Peter 1:18-19

For you know that it was not with perishable things such as silver or gold that you were redeemed from the empty way of life handed down to you from your ancestors, but with the precious blood of Christ.

START Chances are slim that anyone has ever crumbled at your feet and told you how priceless you are. Some days you might feel about as precious as loose change rolling in the gutter. But Jesus prizes you. He considers you so exceedingly valuable that he gave his life so you could live close to him. His sacrifice was infinitely costly. But he counted the cost and gladly laid down everything he had.

Was Jesus a fool to die on the cross for you? Why—or why not?

READ 1 Peter 1:17-21

[17]Since you call on a Father who judges each person's work impartially, live out your time as foreigners here in reverent fear. [18]For you know that it was not with perishable things such as silver or gold that you were redeemed from the empty way of life handed down to you from your ancestors, [19]but with the precious blood of Christ, a lamb without blemish or defect. [20]He was chosen before the creation of the world, but was revealed in these last times for your sake. [21]Through him you believe in God, who raised him from the dead and glorified him, and so your faith and hope are in God.

THINK The apostle Peter—a close follower of Jesus and the author of this Bible passage—just finished explaining that God expects Christians to be holy, that is, to completely dedicate ourselves to God. This passage tells why.

If we're "foreigners," we don't always fit with the world around us. How could living for God make us feel like aliens?

Having "reverent fear" isn't feeling terror toward God but showing appropriate awe. Why live in awe of God?

"Redeem" means paying a price to secure the release of a convicted criminal. What did Jesus redeem us from? What does that mean?

What did it cost Jesus to free you from that "empty way of life"?

No amount of money could cover your purchase price. Because Jesus is God himself, he laid down riches worth more than every human fortune put together. And he paid not just for you but for every human being (1 John 2:2).

LIVE When have people made you feel less-than-valuable?

Jesus paid an infinite price for you. Does that do anything to convince you of your value to him? Why—or why not?

When do you most need to remind yourself of your enormous value to God? How can you do that?

WRAP If you want to know how valuable you are, peek at your price tag. When Jesus went to the cross as payment for you, he settled your worth once and for all. You are exceedingly precious to God.

» MORE THOUGHTS TO MULL

- Do you agree that you needed to be rescued from a worthless way of life? Why—or why not?

- How does Jesus make it possible for you to believe in God? What's the result?

- Make a list of things that are enormously expensive—a beautiful house, a wedding ring, a stunning car, a store filled with beautiful clothes or cutting-edge electronics. Then thank God that you are more valuable than all the fabulous stuff in the world rolled together.

» MORE SCRIPTURES TO DIG

- Like this passage, **Ephesians 1:4** says God's plan to shower goodness on you as his son or daughter—through Jesus—was hatched "before the creation of the world."

- Jesus is called the "Lamb of God" because he died for our sins just as animals were sacrificed for sin in the Old Testament. Read the details in **Hebrews 9**.

- If you ever wonder whether God really wants a relationship with you, Jesus gives you absolute assurance that he does. **Romans 4:25** says Jesus "was handed over to die because of our sins, and he was raised to life to make us right with God" (NLT). Jesus' cross is proof of his love for us, and his resurrection is living proof of his power over sin and death (**Romans 1:4**). And because you've seen Jesus, you can believe in God (**John 1:14; 20:30-31**).

- If you need one more dose of your real value to God, look at **Matthew 27** to see the suffering Jesus went through to buy you back from sin.

4. BACK FROM THE DEAD

You're alive because of God

Ephesians 2:5 (NCV)

Though we were spiritually dead because of the things we did against God, he gave us new life with Christ. You have been saved by God's grace.

START Even though God created people to resemble him (Genesis 1:26), sin makes us a mess. We've each got a disease far worse than a stuffed-up nose. Truth is, spiritually speaking, we're dead. Without God breathing life into us, we do whatever our bodies and minds demand, living only to please ourselves. Ephesians 2:1-2 says, "In the past you were spiritually dead because of your sins and the things you did against God. Yes, in the past you lived the way the world lives" (NCV).

Do you accept what Ephesians 2:1-2 says about you—or not? What kind of person would you be without God's help?

READ Ephesians 2:4-10 (NCV)

> [4] But God's mercy is great, and he loved us very much. [5] Though we were spiritually dead because of the things we did against God, he gave us new life with Christ. You have been saved by God's grace. [6] And he raised us up with Christ and gave us a seat with him in the heavens. He did this for those in Christ Jesus [7] so that for all future time he could show the very great riches of his grace by being kind to us in Christ Jesus. [8] I mean that you have been saved by grace through believing. You did not save yourselves; it was a gift from God. [9] It was not the result of your own efforts, so you cannot brag about it. [10] God has made us what we are. In Christ Jesus, God made us to do good works, which God planned in advance for us to live our lives doing.

THINK The sinful things we think, say, and do make us targets of God's anger (Ephesians 2:3). But God doesn't act on his fury. Why not?

In this passage the opposite of being "dead" is being "saved." What all does it mean to be "saved"?

"Saved" isn't just having a forever home in heaven. It's being made whole, experiencing everything in this passage—receiving God's mercy, getting a new life, enjoying God's kindness, and being set on a good path.

This passage repeats a couple times that we're saved by "grace"—the kindness and favor God shows us even though we don't deserve it. God doesn't save us based on good things we do but because he chooses to be merciful. He saves us when we trust in Jesus and receive the free gift of his forgiveness and everything he has done for us.

What amazes you about grace?

LIVE How have you experienced God saving you?

Have you ever tried to do good so God would love you more? Why can't you get God's love by your own efforts, or what many Bible translations call "works"?

How would your life be different if you really trusted, in every moment, that God's love for you has no strings—and no limits?

WRAP Without God you are spiritually dead. But when you get to know God, he raises you up and gives you new life. It's all because of his grace.

»   MORE THOUGHTS TO MULL

- Why can't any of us brag about being friends with God?

- How would you explain "grace" to a friend who has no idea what it means?

- Make a list of your closest friends. Which friends know about the new life in this passage? How are you helping one another get more and more of that life?

» MORE SCRIPTURES TO DIG

- Grace is one of the Bible's main themes, a one-word description of how God freely loves us. Look at **Titus 2:11-14** to see how God's grace changes your life. Then study how the idea of grace weaves through **Titus 3:5-7**.

- **Ephesians 2:8-10** is one of the most frequently quoted passages in the whole Bible, but you might hear it repeated in different words. Read it in the TNIV translation, then memorize it: "For it is by grace you have been saved, through faith—and this is not from yourselves, it is the gift of God—not by works, so that no one can boast. For we are God's handiwork, created in Christ Jesus to do good works, which God prepared in advance for us to do."

- It's tough to find a better task to add to your to-do list than **2 Peter 3:18**, the last words in that short book: "But grow in the grace and knowledge of our Lord and Savior Jesus Christ. To him be glory both now and forever! Amen."

5. GO AND SIN NO MORE

Jesus will change you forever

John 8:11

"Then neither do I condemn you," Jesus declared. "Go now and leave your life of sin."

START Jesus is teaching in the temple when a group of religious leaders hauls in a woman caught in the act of adultery—that is, having sex with someone other than her spouse. They force the woman to stand in front of the crowd, noting that their laws dictate she should be killed by stoning. When they demand to know if Jesus agrees with them, he doesn't answer. He stoops and writes in the dirt with his finger—maybe doodling, maybe jotting something deep. When Jesus finally stands and speaks, his response stuns them all.

How do you think God treats you when you do something wrong?

READ John 8:7-11

> [7]When they [teachers of the law and the Pharisees] kept on questioning him, he straightened up and said to them, "Let any one of you who is without sin be the first to throw a stone at her." [8]Again he stooped down and wrote on the ground.

> [9]At this, those who heard began to go away one at a time, the older ones first, until only Jesus was left, with the woman still standing there. [10]Jesus straightened up and asked her, "Woman, where are they? Has no one condemned you?"

> [11]"No one, sir," she said.

> "Then neither do I condemn you," Jesus declared. "Go now and leave your life of sin."

THINK The religious leaders don't drag in the man caught in adultery—maybe because all of the accusers were probably male. He, too, was subject to the death penalty (Deuteronomy 22:23-24).

Jesus says the religious leaders can stone the woman, provided they meet one condition. What is it?

What does Jesus imply about the woman's accusers? Why do they all walk away?

Does Jesus think the woman is innocent—or her behavior okay? How do you know?

What two points does Jesus communicate to the woman at the end of this encounter?

LIVE Jesus assures the woman of God's forgiveness. But he also wants her to find freedom from her sin. If you were the woman in this scene, what would you do now?

If God is so ready to forgive sins—even major ones—isn't that an excuse for you to disobey God? Why—or why not?

What motivates you to obey God's commands?

WRAP While no one in this scene disputes the woman's guilt, the religious leaders try to use her situation to trap Jesus. The Lord refuses to exploit her. Or condemn her. He aims to forgive and free her. It's the same way he treats every one of us. He loves us just the way we are. But he loves us too much to leave us that way.

» MORE THOUGHTS TO MULL

- Do you think Jesus let the woman (and her male partner) off easy? Why—or why not?

- Why do you think the woman's older accusers leave first?

- When have you been caught doing wrong—and felt accused and condemned? Have you ever been talked to like Jesus talked to the woman? How would that kind of no-nonsense yet love-filled conversation feel to you?

» MORE SCRIPTURES TO DIG

- Read this whole episode in **John 8:1-11**. You likely will find a note indicating that some manuscripts of John don't contain John 7:53-8:11. Even though this passage isn't found in the oldest copies of John's writings, that doesn't mean the scene isn't real or that it doesn't belong in the Bible. It clearly fits with everything else we see of Jesus in Scripture.

- You might know **John 3:16**, that "God so loved the world that he gave his one and only Son, that whoever believes in him shall not perish but have eternal life." Have a look at **John 3:17-18**, which tells us that God sent his Son into the world to save us, not condemn us.

- The Bible teaches that Satan is "the Accuser," the one who tells us how bad our sins are without telling us how we get God's forgiveness and break free from evil (**Revelation 12:10**). God is nothing like him. When God needs to point out something we're doing wrong—through the Bible, through the correction of others, or through our own consciences—he does it for our good. He assures us of his love and helps us change. Like **Romans 8:1** says, "There is now no condemnation for those who are in Christ Jesus."

6. DO OVERS

You can get fresh starts

1 John 1:8-9

If we claim to be without sin, we deceive ourselves and the truth is not in us. If we confess our sins, he is faithful and just and will forgive us our sins and purify us from all unrighteousness.

START Having the courage to admit you've sinned is core to being a Christian. It's how you start in faith. It's also how you keep going after you've messed up. This next passage comes near the beginning of 1 John, a short letter written by the same close friend of Jesus who wrote the much longer Gospel of John. You can't help but sense this guy is intensely grateful to get hold of God's always-available forgiveness. But he's equally passionate about challenging his readers to break free from sin and thrive in every bit of life.

How easily do you admit you're wrong? Examples, please.

READ 1 John 1:8-2:2

> ¹:⁸If we claim to be without sin, we deceive ourselves and the truth is not in us. ⁹If we confess our sins, he is faithful and just and will forgive us our sins and purify us from all unrighteousness. ¹⁰If we claim we have not sinned, we make him out to be a liar and his word is not in us.
>
> ²:¹ My dear children, I write this to you so that you will not sin. But if anybody does sin, we have an advocate with the Father—Jesus Christ, the Righteous One. ²He is the atoning sacrifice for our sins, and not only for ours but also for the sins of the whole world.

THINK What's the problem with saying we don't sin—or that our sins aren't so bad?

Suppose you just did something wrong. What does God want you to do? What two things does he promise to do in response?

To "confess" literally means "to say the same thing." It's admitting that your sin is sin, as wrong as God says it is.

Why does God forgive you? What does that mean?

Why is John writing? And how is Jesus able to help us when we mess up?

Jesus is our defender as he sits at his Father's right hand. He advocates for us like an always-present lawyer, making our case in the court that matters most. He is the "atoning sacrifice" who takes the punishment for our sin and reconciles us to God.

LIVE Why would you want to break free from sin? How does sin keep you from thriving in life?

How do you react when you realize you've sinned? Are you more likely to start fresh or to stubbornly keep doing wrong? Why?

What do you want to do differently next time you realize you've done wrong?

WRAP Admitting your sin is the first step in grabbing hold of God's forgiveness and keeping close to him. So keep two facts in your head: Fact 1: Even as a Christian you sin, and sin strains your relationships with God and people. Fact 2: You have God's promise that if you confess your wrongs, God forgives. After all, Christians aren't people who never fall down; they're the ones who get up and go on.

» MORE THOUGHTS TO MULL

- Some Christians have difficulty believing God forgives them for messing up, even when they admit they've done wrong. If that's you, find a wise older Christian to share your doubts with.

- Think of the Christians you know. Who is swift to admit they're wrong and quick to get back up when they've fallen down? What can you learn from them?

- How do you keep from leaping into sin when you know God has promised to forgive you?

» **MORE SCRIPTURES TO DIG**

- God won't break his word. So when you confess your sins to him, your sins are *gone*. Like **Psalm 103:12** says, "He has taken our sins away from us as far as the east is from west" (NCV).

- Most people never ponder how we fail to measure up to God's absolute goodness. Like high school basketball hotshots, we think we can play center in the NBA—until we stand next to an opponent just shy of eight feet tall. When we get to know God, he starts remaking us. But, this side of heaven, we won't ever be totally unflawed. Doubt that? See how you measure up against the lists of right and wrong in **Ephesians 4:25-5:4** or **Galatians 5:19-21**.

- Read on in **1 John 2:1-6**. If you keep on sinning nonstop, that may mean you haven't really understood the greatness of God's kind forgiveness. Or maybe you don't know that God wants not only to forgive you but also to change you. If you find yourself trapped over and over by sin, ask God to help you figure out what's going on inside you. And remember that he's made an unbreakable promise: Jesus is the sacrifice that paid for your sins.

- God's work in you is never finished. **Philippians 1:6** says that when you become a Christian, God starts changing and growing you. He won't stop until he's done.

7. LOVE UNLIMITED

You are wildly loved

Romans 8:38-39

For I am convinced that neither death nor life, neither angels nor demons, neither the present nor the future, nor any powers, neither height nor depth, nor anything else in all creation, will be able to separate us from the love of God that is in Christ Jesus our Lord.

START You can't thrive without God's never-ending love any more than a flower can burst open without soil, sun, and rain. God accepts you, lifts you from death, assures you of your great value, and lets you start over again and again. But there's more. He tops it all off with his moment-by-moment care that reaches every dark place of your life. It's a fact: When you meet God you get a wild love you can't get anywhere else.

When have you felt deep pain—and feared you were all alone in your agony? How did you count on God in that situation—or not?

READ Romans 8:31-39

[31]What, then, shall we say in response to these things? If God is for us, who can be against us? [32]He who did not spare his own Son, but gave him up for us all—how will he not also, along with him, graciously give us all things? [33]Who will bring any charge against those whom God has chosen? It is God who justifies. [34]Who then can condemn? No one. Christ Jesus who died—more than that, who was raised to life—is at the right hand of God and is also interceding for us. [35]Who shall separate us from the love of Christ? Shall trouble or hardship or persecution or famine or nakedness or danger or sword? [36]As it is written: "For your sake we face death all day long; we are considered as sheep to be slaughtered." [37]No, in all these things we are more than conquerors through him who loved us. [38]For I am convinced that neither death nor life, neither angels nor demons, neither the present nor the future, nor any powers, [39]neither height nor depth, nor anything else in all creation, will be able to separate us from the love of God that is in Christ Jesus our Lord.

THINK God is so much on our side that he gave his Son for us. What does that prove?

God justifies us—makes us right with him. What good does that do?

Jot down all the things mentioned in this passage that can't stop God's love for you.

God's love doesn't guarantee you'll always escape tough stuff in life. What does it mean that we are "more than conquerors"?

LIVE This Bible passage unfurls a long list of things that can't stop God's love. Make your own real-world list of the toughest things you face. Which ones can thwart his love for you?

How is God's love unlike the love people can give you?

How can you be sure God loves you even when terrible things happen?

WRAP Psalm 36:5-6 declares, "Your love, Lord, reaches to the heavens, your faithfulness to the skies. Your righteousness is like the highest mountains, your justice like the great deep." God's love is one-of-a-kind. It's bigger than anything you will battle.

》 MORE THOUGHTS TO MULL

- When have tough circumstances made you question God's love for you? What answers have you discovered?

- Why is being certain of God's love crucial to thriving in life?

- Find a friend, and share these encouraging words from Romans 8:31-39 with that person.

» MORE SCRIPTURES TO DIG

- Have a look at **Ephesians 3:14-21**, where the apostle Paul prays you would grasp how incredibly wide and long and high and deep is God's love for you.

- Chances are you know people who think God is infuriated with the universe and won't be satisfied until he destroys us all. Check out these passages that tell you about your loving Lord: **Psalm 145**, **Lamentations 3:22-23**, **1 John 4:7-19**.

- The passage you read wraps up **Romans 8**, one of the Bible's most amazing chapters. The apostle Paul starts by explaining how the Holy Spirit helps you overcome sin (**8:1-17**). It coaches us to endure whatever difficulties we face as Christians, because our sufferings are nothing compared to the great life God has for us in heaven (**8:18-27**). Then it informs us that God works for our good no matter how bad our situation looks (**8:28-30**).

8. OPEN-DOOR POLICY

You can get close to God

Hebrews 10:19

We have confidence to enter the Most Holy Place by the blood of Jesus.

START Before Jesus came on the scene, Old Testament people drew close to God primarily at the temple in Jerusalem. The temple's innermost room—the Most Holy Place—was as close as anyone could get. Only once a year did God allow the chief priest to slip through a curtain into this special place of God's presence. The priest's position didn't get him in. Neither did ornate prayers or secret passwords. He entered carrying the blood of goats and calves sacrificed for the sins of the people (Hebrews 9:12). When Jesus offered himself as the perfect sacrifice for sin, he became our way to get close to God.

Describe what it looks and feels like to live close to God—right here, right now.

READ Hebrews 10:19-23

> [19]Therefore, brothers and sisters, since we have confidence to enter the Most Holy Place by the blood of Jesus, [20]by a new and living way opened for us through the curtain, that is, his body, [21]and since we have a great priest over the house of God, [22]let us draw near to God with a sincere heart in full assurance of faith, having our hearts sprinkled to cleanse us from a guilty conscience and having our bodies washed with pure water. [23]Let us hold unswervingly to the hope we profess, for he who promised is faithful.

THINK The "blood of Jesus" isn't bottled magic. It's a quick term that refers to Jesus' death on the cross. What exactly did Jesus' sacrifice open up for you?

When Jesus died on the cross, the curtain blocking the way to the Most Holy Place tore in two from heaven to earth (Matthew 27:51). That's a vivid symbol that God forever ripped open a way to himself that no one can sew shut.

The fact that Jesus is the "great priest over the house of God" means he brought the right sacrifice to God. So how can you enter God's presence because of him? Spot at least three descriptions in this short passage.

Having our "hearts sprinkled" and our "bodies washed" refers to the cleansing that takes place when God makes us his friends. We stand spotless before God, our sins completely washed away. That's why we can enter confidently, without fear.

Why can we count on these facts?

LIVE When have you noticed that sin makes you feel distant from God?

Do you think it's unfair that you need Christ's death to truly get close to God? Why—or why not?

How will the sacrifice of Jesus change how you relate to God today?

WRAP We can relate to God without fear as long as we keep fresh in our minds the facts of what Jesus did for us. He opened a door no one can ever shut. Check how Ephesians 3:12 sums it up: "Because of Christ and our faith in him, we can now come boldly and confidently into God's presence" (NLT). That promise is good for now and forever. It lets you talk to God with total confidence.

»   MORE THOUGHTS TO MULL

- Why is God so particular about who gets close to him?

- Ask three people to tell you how they think they can get God to like them.

- If the blood of Jesus is what gets you close to God, what is the point of habits like praying or reading your Bible?

» MORE SCRIPTURES TO DIG

- Jesus not only pulls us close to God but to one another. Look at what the author of Hebrews says in the verses that come right after our main passage: "And let us consider how we may spur one another on toward love and good deeds, not giving up meeting together, as some are in the habit of doing, but encouraging one another..." (**Hebrews 10:24-25**).

- God might seem harsh about who is let into his presence. But remember that sinning against God isn't just dissing a friend. It's disrespecting the Lord of the universe. God sees sin for what it really is—an ultimate choice against him, an infinite crime with an infinite penalty. Like **Psalm 5:4** says, "For you are not a God who is pleased with wickedness; with you, evil people are not welcome." God has zero tolerance for sin, but he was so saddened by our separation from him that he sent Jesus to die so we could get close to him again.

- Maybe you think hanging out with God sounds like as much fun as spending time with a cranky old neighbor. Not so. **Psalm 16:11** says, "You will fill me with joy in your presence." Read **Psalm 84** for a stunning description of living tight with God.

9. GO TO GOD

Your best friend understands your struggles

Hebrews 4:16

Let us then approach God's throne of grace with confidence, so that we may receive mercy and find grace to help us in our time of need.

START God possesses total knowledge. But if you've ever wondered if God really knows and understands everything you go through, Jesus' coming to earth in human flesh (John 1:14) offers you proof that his all-knowing brain has real in-the-body experience. Going to God won't do you any good if he roars at your problems and orders you to clean up your mess by yourself. The last Bible passage showed how you can come to God. This one shows why you want to.

How ready is Jesus to lend a hand when you need help? What's your evidence or examples?

READ Hebrews 4:13-16

> [13]Nothing in all creation is hidden from God's sight. Everything is uncovered and laid bare before the eyes of him to whom we must give account.
>
> [14]Therefore, since we have a great high priest who has ascended into heaven, Jesus the Son of God, let us hold firmly to the faith we profess. [15]For we do not have a high priest who is unable to empathize with our weaknesses, but we have one who has been tempted in every way, just as we are—yet he did not sin. [16]Let us then approach God's throne of grace with confidence, so that we may receive mercy and find grace to help us in our time of need.

THINK If God knows everything about us—and there's nothing we can hide from him—how should we act when we're near him?

Why doesn't Jesus criticize us for being weak?

You don't have to read much of the Old Testament to notice that people were into gigantic evil—from child sacrifice to idol worship, incest, and witchcraft. Life didn't get any prettier in the New Testament. Writing to the Christians in Corinth, Paul mentions sins like sexual immorality, idolatry, stealing, greed, drunkenness, and slander—noting that some members of that church had once been quite involved in such activity (1 Corinthians 6:9-11). So when this passage asserts that Jesus gets what we go through and understands the kind of sin that surrounds us in this world, you can be sure those aren't empty words.

What do you receive from God when you go to him?

"Mercy" is God's tender grasp of your situation and his ability to unleash whatever it takes to take care of you. "Grace" is his unearned favor and for-giveness you've already heard about. Roll the two together, and it means that God will give you exactly what you need.

LIVE If you could tell God about one area where you need his mercy and grace—what would you tell him?

What subjects do you want to avoid discussing with God? Why?

Do you think Jesus actually understands your temptations and other problems? Why—or why not?

Jesus faced even fiercer battles than the rest of us humans. We usually lose hope, give up, and dive into sin before the fight gets truly grueling. Jesus remained true to God's commands his whole life. But he didn't have it easy.

WRAP God understands your every need, whether it's help with your homework or freedom from sins that overpower you. Ponder these words from a classic worship song: "He walked where I walk. He stood where I stand. He felt what I feel. He understands."

» MORE THOUGHTS TO MULL

- Suppose a friend has a dark secret no one knows. What would you say to convince him or her it's safe to talk to God?

- When you try to explain a problem to someone, how much does it matter if they've actually gone through whatever it is you face? Explain.

- How could someone who never sinned really know how bad it can get while battling to do the right thing?

» MORE SCRIPTURES TO DIG

- The famous Old Testament king David writes in **Psalm 139:1-3**, "You have searched me, LORD, and you know me. You know when I sit and when I rise; you perceive my thoughts from afar. You discern my going out and my lying down; you are familiar with all my ways." The all-knowing God might sound terrifying, but David actually invites God to examine him. "Search me, God, and know my heart," he says at the end of the song, "test me and know my anxious thoughts. See if there is any offensive way in me, and lead me in the way everlasting" (**Psalm 139:23-24**).

- The Bible teaches that Jesus, at the end of his time on this planet, "ascended" to heaven (**Acts 1:9-11**). He didn't just drift away on a cloud. Jesus came to earth on a mission, and "after he had provided purification for sins, he sat down at the right hand of the Majesty in heaven" (**Hebrews 1:3**). He's now back in the control center of the universe, forever on your side—living proof that your sins are forgiven (**1 John 2:1-2**).

- Think of an area where you need God's help. Use a concordance, Bible study software, topical Bible, or another Christian's wisdom to find verses that give you the information and encouragement you need.

10. GET IT TOGETHER

You're part of a family

Acts 2:42

They devoted themselves to the apostles' teaching and to fellowship, to the breaking of bread and to prayer.

START If you can imagine every Christian you know suddenly getting passionate about God in every part of life, then you get a small glimpse of what happened during the birth of the church. After Jesus left earth for heaven, the Holy Spirit came and enabled believers to worship God in languages they'd never learned. Hostile onlookers thought the scene was so weird they accused the believers of an early morning drinking binge. A very sober Peter seizes the chance to tell the whole Jesus story—that God had raised Jesus from the dead, and they had all seen the risen Jesus with their own eyes. Then he hits his hearers with one last fact: The Jesus they nailed to the cross is both Lord and Savior (Acts 2:1-36).

What would it look like if you and all your friends decided to live totally for God?

READ Acts 2:42-47

> [42]They devoted themselves to the apostles' teaching and to fellowship, to the breaking of bread and to prayer. [43]Everyone was filled with awe at the many wonders and signs performed by the apostles. [44]All the believers were together and had everything in common. [45]They sold property and possessions to give to anyone who had need. [46]Every day they continued to meet together in the temple courts. They broke bread in their homes and ate together with glad and sincere hearts, [47]praising God and enjoying the favor of all the people. And the Lord added to their number daily those who were being saved.

THINK What habits kept the early Christians busy?

Don't picture these disciples as crazed fanatics who were simply riding a wave of emotion. Sure, they had discovered that their crucified Lord was alive. And 3,000 people had just become Christians (Acts 2:41). Yet "devoted" means the new disciples applied "a steadfast and single-minded fidelity to a certain course of action." "Breaking of bread" might simply refer to eating together—an even more significant sign of community in that culture than in ours—or it might mean a sacred meal like Communion. The term for "prayer" means making requests to God, coupled with praise.

What else were the apostles doing?

Jesus promised that his followers would do miracles even more spectacular than what he did (John 14:12). Notice that the disciples' awe came even before the spectacular signs. We don't have to wait for God to do a fresh miracle to realize he's real. Miracles don't get any more stunning than Christ's resurrection.

Who liked what was going on? What was the result?

LIVE What changes do you expect to see in yourself and others when you follow God?

Why were the early Christians having such a good time? How is that like or unlike church as you know it?

If someone who doesn't believe in Jesus came to your church, what would she see to make her want to stick around?

WRAP When the crowds heard Peter's sermon about the crucifixion and resurrection of Jesus, they felt stabbing pain: "When the people heard this, they felt guilty and asked Peter and the other apostles, 'What shall we do?'" (Acts 2:37, NCV). Peter told them to quit sinning, be forgiven, testify to their new faith by being baptized, and let God live close to them through the Holy Spirit. It's what God is working to do in you, too.

» MORE THOUGHTS TO MULL

- How were the early Christians like family to one another?

- What keeps us from developing the passionate commitment of the early Christians?

- Ask a mature Christian what things might be holding you back from a spiritual growth spurt.

» MORE SCRIPTURES TO DIG

- Jesus promised his followers would be filled with the Holy Spirit in **Luke 24:49** and **Acts 1:4-8**.

- Check out all of **Acts 2** for the big picture of the birth of the church. Peter explained that everything the crowds saw and heard on the religious holiday of Pentecost was a fulfillment of an Old Testament prophecy you can read in **Joel 2:28-29**.

- Read **Acts 3** for more of Peter's preaching in those early days of the church.

- Like these earliest Christians who sold their possessions to provide for others in need, sincere Christians throughout history have struggled to live counter to prevailing culture by living simply and using their wealth to benefit the needy, both in their midst and around the world. The Bible encourages us to give generously and willingly (**2 Corinthians 9:6-7**). By strategically and sacrificially sharing, we can change our world (**2 Corinthians 9:12-15**).

11. PLUGGED IN

You have a new power source

John 14:16-17

I will ask the Father, and he will give you another advocate to help you and be with you forever—the Spirit of truth.

START Thriving isn't just about what God has done for you—giving you a radically new life—but also about what he is doing in you right now. God wants to power you up and give you everything you need to reach the goals he has in mind for you. As a Christian you're designed to draw on the endless energy supply of God's Holy Spirit. In this passage Jesus details for his followers how the Spirit—the "advocate" or the "Spirit of truth"—works in us.

What kind of power do you expect from God to help you in everyday life? How exactly do you get that help?

READ John 14:15-21

> [15]"If you love me, keep my commands. [16]And I will ask the Father, and he will give you another advocate to help you and be with you forever— [17]the Spirit of truth. The world cannot accept him, because it neither sees him nor knows him. But you know him, for he lives with you and will be in you. [18]I will not leave you as orphans; I will come to you. [19]Before long, the world will not see me anymore, but you will see me. Because I live, you also will live. [20]On that day you will realize that I am in my Father, and you are in me, and I am in you. [21]Whoever has my commands and keeps them is the one who loves me. Anyone who loves me will be loved by my Father, and I too will love them and show myself to them."

THINK How do we show we love Jesus? What's the result of loving him?

Remember? Obeying God doesn't make us acceptable to him. Yet obeying is how we show our gratitude. When we obey we see more of God. Like in any friendship, we won't feel connected to God if we've got our backs to him.

Where will the "advocate" live? For how long?

The word for "advocate" literally means "a person summoned to one's aid." It can also be translated as "counselor" and can refer to an advisor or mediator. Because you have the Holy Spirit—as all Christians do (1 John 4:13)—God doesn't just watch over you but is in you, "indwelling" you through his Spirit.

What will the advocate do for you?

Other New Testament passages fill out the picture: The Spirit teaches you (John 14:26), gives you and other Christians spiritual gifts to help one another grow (1 Corinthians 12, 14), guides you (Romans 8:1-27), empowers you to tell others about Christ (Acts 1:8), and remakes your attitudes and actions to look like Jesus (Galatians 5:16-25).

LIVE Describe what it means to thrive—to become the person Jesus wants you to be.

How do you expect the Holy Spirit to help you get to that good place?

What do you want to do today to plug into the Spirit's strength?

WRAP Do you want more of the Spirit in your life? Then listen up for what the Spirit tries to teach you each day through the Bible, other Christians, and simple whispers of how to do right and stay close to God. Like Galatians 5:25 says, "Since we are living by the Spirit, let us follow the Spirit's leading in every part of our lives" (NLT).

» MORE THOUGHTS TO MULL

- Jesus was God in a human body. But like any other human being, he could be in only one place at any particular time. So how would it be easier or harder to follow Jesus if he were living somewhere on earth right now?

- Ask a mature Christian how the Holy Spirit helps us get closer to God.

- Tell God you want his Spirit to work in you. Then let him.

» MORE SCRIPTURES TO DIG

- Throughout his life Jesus talked about his supremely close relationship with his "Father." He wasn't talking about Joseph, his earthly dad, but his Father in heaven. Jesus declared that he and the Father were so close they were "one" (**John 10:30**). Here in **John 14** as well as in **John 16:5-15** he adds another twist, promising that when he leaves earth he and the Father will send an "advocate" to be with his followers. Jesus implies that he and this advocate are different, yet so closely connected that they are somehow the same.

- Jesus wasn't talking about something entirely new when he brought up the Holy Spirit. It was the "Spirit of God" that hovered over the water in the first verse of the Bible, **Genesis 1:2**. Hundreds of years before Jesus, the prophet Joel had prophesied the Spirit's powerful arrival (**Joel 2:28-32**). Yet the first Christians debated for years exactly how to interpret what Jesus explained about God. God is a "Trinity"—not three separate Gods but a "tri-unity," one being (God) in three persons (Father, Son, and Holy Spirit). This truth might be hard to understand—in fact, just the idea that Jesus and the Father were one confused the disciples. Yet if we want to make sense of the Bible, this is a truth we need to get hold of.

12. PURE SATISFACTION

You'll get everything you really need

Philippians 4:12-13

I have learned the secret of being content in any and every situation, whether well fed or hungry, whether living in plenty or in want. I can do all this through him who gives me strength.

START The apostle Paul suffered everything from imprisonments to stoning to shipwrecks in order to tell the world about Jesus (2 Corinthians 11:21-33). He knew he had a right to get paid for his preaching (1 Timothy 5:18), yet he hated asking for help from the people he taught about God (1 Thessalonians 2:9). So how did he get by? He kept fed by making tents (Acts 18:3). That all might sound super-tough, like he wanted to make it through life all by himself. But even Paul needed the encouragement and support of close friends.

Who do you trust to take care of you—even if everyone else in the world lets you down? What all do you expect from that person?

READ Philippians 4:10-13

[10]I rejoiced greatly in the Lord that at last you renewed your concern for me. Indeed, you were concerned, but you had no opportunity to show it. [11]I am not saying this because I am in need, for I have learned to be content whatever the circumstances. [12]I know what it is to be in need, and I know what it is to have plenty. I have learned the secret of being content in any and every situation, whether well fed or hungry, whether living in plenty or in want. [13]I can do all this through him who gives me strength.

THINK How do you know Paul wasn't holding his breath waiting for money to arrive from the believers in Philippi? How does Paul manage to survive anything life throws at him?

Who does Paul count on to take care of him?

Paul realizes that while God is the ultimate source of every good gift, God's care often comes through people. Paul expresses appreciation for the kind gifts from his Philippian friends, yet he's also content to rely on God for his needs.

Picture Paul waking up day after day to do ministry—some good days, some desperate and dangerous days. What does Paul expect God to do for him?

LIVE Name your biggest needs in these areas or others: School...friend-ships...spiritual growth...money...activities like sports or music...getting along at home.

What does God have to do with meeting those needs?

How would you respond to someone who thinks he doesn't need people—or that he doesn't need God?

Paul finishes his comments—and his letter—with an amazing promise to the Philippians, a promise that applies to us as well: "My God will meet all your needs according to the riches of his glory in Christ Jesus" (4:19). But how does that work? Why don't you always get what you ask God for?

WRAP Paul looked to God to meet his every need. His words also imply there's a difference between wants and needs. God promises that you'll get whatever you really need to get you where you're going.

» MORE THOUGHTS TO MULL

- How can you cultivate Paul's attitude of contentment in your own life?

- How can Paul claim to be so massively strong when anyone watching him from the outside would say he's totally weak?

- Pray today for each thing on your biggest-needs list. Tell God you trust him to take care of you.

» MORE SCRIPTURES TO DIG

- Paul doesn't nail down exactly what he means by "living in plenty." He might be looking back to the time when he was a leader among the Jewish people (**Galatians 1:14**). Or he might have been thinking way more downscale. He once wrote, "But if we have food and clothing, we will be content with that" (**1 Timothy 6:8**).

- Verses 13 and 19 of Philippians 4 are two of the most famous verses in the Bible. Paul wrote well-known passages elsewhere about being strong even when he felt exceedingly weak. Check **2 Corinthians 4:7-11** and **12:7-10** for more of Paul's amazing insights.

- Look at **Psalm 145:14-19** and **James 1:17** for more on how God provides for your needs.

13. SIMPLY AMAZING

You are gifted

Ephesians 4:11-12

So Christ himself gave the apostles, the prophets, the evangelists, the pastors and teachers, to equip his people for works of service, so that the body of Christ may be built up.

START The apostle Paul was thinking of you when he wrote, "A spiritual gift is given to each of us" (1 Corinthians 12:7, NLT). That news might shock you, especially when the gifts you spot in the Bible range from serving and teaching to doing miracles and speaking in languages you don't learn in school. When you hear that God has given you a gift to help other Christians mature, you might feel confident—you've been taught plenty about spiritual gifts. You might feel confused—absolutely clueless. Or you might be curious—wanting to know more. However you feel, there's no doubt about you or any other believer: You are amazingly gifted.

What do you think about the news that you have a spiritual gift? How does it make you feel?

READ Ephesians 4:11-16

> [11]So Christ himself gave the apostles, the prophets, the evangelists, the pastors and teachers, [12]to equip his people for works of service, so that the body of Christ may be built up [13]until we all reach unity in the faith and in the knowledge of the Son of God and become mature, attaining to the whole measure of the fullness of Christ.
>
> [14]Then we will no longer be infants, tossed back and forth by the waves, and blown here and there by every wind of teaching and by the cunning and craftiness of people in their deceitful scheming. [15]Instead, speaking the truth in love, we will in all things grow up into him who is the head, that is, Christ. [16]From him the whole body, joined and held together by every supporting ligament, grows and builds itself up in love, as each part does its work.

THINK What goal does God have for his people when he equips us with his gifts?

The gifts Paul lists in Ephesians 4 all sound like up-front leadership abilities. Paul details many other spiritual gifts in 1 Corinthians 12:7-11 and Romans 12:4-8, ranging from practical helpfulness to warm hospitality to a knack for encouraging others. Many Bible scholars think the Bible's long and varied lists are only samples of the ways God gifts people. So don't be afraid to use these spiritual gifts—and all of your unique interests and abilities—to help others go deeper with God.

What will happen if we don't put our gifts into action?

What does love have to do with using our spiritual gifts?

LIVE When have you been able to help others know God better? What did you do? How did God give you the ability to help?

Look at this list of spiritual gifts pulled from the New Testament passages listed above: Serving, teaching, encouragement, giving, leading, showing mercy, wisdom, knowledge, faith, healing, miracles, prophecy, distinguishing between good and evil spirits, speaking in tongues, interpretation of tongues, apostleship, evangelism, pastoring. Can you spot yourself in any of those gifts? If not, what other gifts do you think you might have?

How could putting your spiritual gift into action help you discover something fresh about yourself and make your faith feel utterly significant? How could using your gift help others thrive?

WRAP Some of the spiritual gifts listed in the Bible look spectacular. Others look completely everydayish. But all of them take you above and beyond what you can do on your own. Invite God to show you your gifts—and to use you in ways that will boggle your mind.

» MORE THOUGHTS TO MULL

- How have you seen other Christians using their spiritual gifts?

- If you want help figuring out your spiritual gifts, talk to your pastor or another mature Christian. Or pick up the book *Find Your Fit* by Jane Kise and Kevin Johnson (Bethany House, 1998). It shows how your talents, spiritual gifts, and personality all add up to you.

- Being able to identify your gift is far less important than getting involved. Start doing something for God and you'll begin to discover what talents and gifts God gave you. So how can you start to serve him today?

» MORE SCRIPTURES TO DIG

- Spiritual gifts can be controversial. Paul needed all of **1 Corinthians 12-14** to correct his readers' confusion about these gifts. He highlights how love and proper use of the Spirit's gifts glorify God.

- Make sure you check **1 Corinthians 12:7-11** and **Romans 12:4-8** as well as the verses before and after those passages to catch the context of the Bible's teachings on spiritual gifts.

- Don't miss **1 Corinthians 12:12-31**, where Paul explains that each one of us is necessary for the church to function. We're all part of the body of Christ. When parts go missing, the body breaks down.

14. THE PLAN

God is working for your good

Romans 8:28

We know that in all things God works for the good of those who love him, who have been called according to his purpose.

START You can bet that when your life feels like a multi-car pileup—the kind of crash where you get ejected through the windshield and wake up crumpled in a ditch—that's the moment when people will show up, saying things like "Something good will come out of it" and "It must have happened for a reason." Not so sure? You're normal.

Do you expect positive outcomes when bad things happen? Does every dark cloud have a silver lining? What evidence can you offer?

READ Romans 8:28-30

> [28]And we know that in all things God works for the good of those who love him, who have been called according to his purpose. [29]For those God foreknew he also predestined to be conformed to the image of his Son, that he might be the firstborn among many brothers and sisters. [30]And those he predestined, he also called; those he called, he also justified; those he justified, he also glorified.

THINK Right before those verses the apostle Paul explains that because of human sin "the whole creation has been groaning as in the pains of childbirth right up to the present time" (Romans 8:22). Translation: The planet is messed up. Pain happens.

What does God promise to do no matter what happens in life? Who is that promise for?

The point isn't that "bad things are good" or even that "bad things turn out good," but that God works for our good whether life goes great or ghastly. While God does good to people whether they love him or not—whether they are good or evil (Matthew 5:45)—this verse says God has something special in store for those who belong to him.

What purpose does God want to accomplish as he works on our behalf—that is, what does he plan for us to become?

God does often rescue us from bad scenes. But maybe you've never heard that God's overarching plan for your life isn't to make you exquisitely comfortable. It's to make you like Jesus (to "be conformed to the image of his Son"). Here's what happens:

- God wants to produce in you qualities like "love, joy, peace, patience, kindness, goodness, faithfulness, gentleness and self-control" (Galatians 5:22-23).

- You endure some rough bumps in order to grow in character (Romans 5:1-4).

- You become part of a long-term process. You're called—chosen in Christ. You're justified—made right with him. And you're glorified—transformed to think like him (Romans 12:2), act like him (2 Corinthians 3:18), and one day even get a heavenly body like his (Philippians 3:21).

If you think the word *glorified* sounds a little grand for the life you're living now, you're right. We groan while we wait for this transformation to happen (Romans 8:23).

LIVE Say it in your own words: What kind of good is God working for in your life?

Suppose something terrible happens to you. What do you expect God to do?

Do you like God's goal for you? Why—or why not?

WRAP This passage wraps together huge ideas. But they tell you what God wants you to be. You know what he's trying to do in you. You know he's on your side. It's all part of his plan for you to thrive.

»   MORE THOUGHTS TO MULL

- Do you wish God had promised to always rescue you from harm? Why—or why not?

- As you studied this passage, what changed in your understanding of what God is up to in your life?

- List the three worst things that have ever happened to you. Don't pretend that bad things are good—but answer these questions: What good did God work for you—and in you? Are you any more like Jesus?

»   **MORE SCRIPTURES TO DIG**

- The first verse in this Bible passage contains words someone might toss your way when life gets vicious—"we know that all things work together for good to them that love God" (**Romans 8:28, KJV**). That's a less-than-best translation of the Greek in which the Bible was originally written. God doesn't magically make a bad thing good. Instead, he works for your real good in the midst of even the worst situations.

- **Psalm 18:2** packs into a single verse six different names that describe how God rescues his people from harm. God is your "rock," "fortress," "deliverer," "shield," "salvation," and "stronghold." But the ultimate way God rescues you and does you good is to conform you to the likeness of his Son.

15. UPPER HAND

You can beat temptation

Matthew 4:4

Jesus answered, "It is written: 'People do not live on bread alone, but on every word that comes from the mouth of God.'"

START Say "Jesus" and the first thing that pops into some people's minds are words like weak or wimpy—or worse. They assume this good guy must be a mama's boy. But Jesus never had it easy. Recall that he was "tempted in every way, just as we are—yet he did not sin" (Hebrews 4:15). His battles were meaner than anything we've faced or will ever face, and he is tougher than we can imagine.

What would you say to someone who claims Jesus is a wimp—or that faith is for the weak?

READ Matthew 4:1-11

[1] Then Jesus was led by the Spirit into the wilderness to be tempted by the devil. [2] After fasting forty days and forty nights, he was hungry. [3] The tempter came to him and said, "If you are the Son of God, tell these stones to become bread."

[4] Jesus answered, "It is written: 'People do not live on bread alone, but on every word that comes from the mouth of God.'"

[5] Then the devil took him to the holy city and had him stand on the highest point of the temple. [6] "If you are the Son of God," he said, "throw yourself down. For it is written: 'He will command his angels concerning you, and they will lift you up in their hands, so that you will not strike your foot against a stone.'"

[7] Jesus answered him, "It is also written: 'Do not put the Lord your God to the test.'"

[8] Again, the devil took him to a very high mountain and showed him all the kingdoms of the world and their splendor. [9] "All this I will give you," he said, "if you will bow down and worship me."

¹⁰Jesus said to him, "Away from me, Satan! For it is written: 'Worship the Lord your God, and serve him only.'"

¹¹Then the devil left him, and angels came and attended him.

THINK When Satan shows up to tempt Jesus, what has Jesus been doing—or not doing—for forty days? What's that first temptation all about?

After Jesus had spent more than a month going without food to devote himself to prayer, Satan suggests he miraculously bake himself some bread. Satan tries a classic ploy, urging Jesus to meet legitimate needs in a sinful way, outside of God's plan. It's the same trick he tries on us, like when he tries to convince us to engage in sex outside of marriage. Sex is a good gift straight from God—but not when we dive in at the wrong place and time.

Surprisingly, Jesus doesn't wave an all-powerful finger at Satan and smoke him. How does Jesus fight back?

When Satan urges Jesus to dive off the temple's peak, the temptation is for Jesus to win popularity with a powerful yet pointless miracle. Then Satan takes Jesus to a mountaintop to try to swing a deal. What does Satan promise Jesus? On what condition?

What truth does Jesus use to drive Satan away?

LIVE How surprised are you that Jesus was genuinely tempted to do wrong just like you? Explain.

You've already heard that Jesus lived in a crude yet enticing world. Yet in every moment and every situation of life, he stayed faithful to God's commands. He made the tough choice instead of taking the easy way out by conforming to his surroundings.

How do you want to handle the next temptation that comes your way?

WRAP When you feel tempted, you have access to the same source of strength Jesus used: God's Word. God has outfitted you with the world's most powerful temptation blaster—the true facts of life found in the Bible.

» MORE THOUGHTS TO MULL

- When you feel tempted do you usually fight back—or give in? Why?

- Think of an area where you face frequent temptation. Ask a mature Christian to help you find Scriptures that help you battle back.

- Fighting temptation doesn't have to be a solo battle. Who can help you conquer your biggest sins?

» MORE SCRIPTURES TO DIG

- This scene might strike you as strange, but here's what's going on. Right before Jesus was about to begin his full-time ministry, the Holy Spirit led him to a place where he could fellowship with his Father. But along with that closeness, Jesus also experienced colossal temptation to become the world's Savior without going to the cross. While God himself never tempts anyone (**James 1:13**), Jesus is getting the chance to prove he's as obedient under intense pressure as he is in normal life.

- Temptation doesn't always come straight from Satan. Often it's the dark underside of our hearts that gets us craving wrong things (**James 1:14-15**).

- **1 Corinthians 10:13** offers you this bright promise: "No temptation has overtaken you except what is common to us all. And God is faithful; he will not let you be tempted beyond what you can bear. But when you are tempted, he will also provide a way out so that you can endure it." Memorize that verse. Then build a habit of looking for God's way out of sin.

16. TRUE FAITH

You are tougher than any trial

1 Peter 1:6-7

In all this you greatly rejoice, though now for a little while you may have had to suffer grief in all kinds of trials. These have come so that your faith—of greater worth than gold, which perishes even though refined by fire— may be proved genuine and may result in praise, glory and honor when Jesus Christ is revealed.

START The Bible doesn't pretend to dish out easy answers to life's worst pains. The peace we want from God isn't always easy to find. Yet in a letter to churches scattered across what is now Turkey, the apostle Peter tells a group of people who are being attacked for their faith how to triumph when tough times come. Scholars debate exactly what Peter's readers are facing, though we can spot in 1 Peter 3:8-17 and 4:12-19 that they are suffering for doing right. We also know that deadly persecution against Christians is a mere year or two away in Rome, where Peter is likely living as he writes.

Have you ever suffered for your faith? How did you respond?

READ 1 Peter 1:3-9

> [3]Praise be to the God and Father of our Lord Jesus Christ! In his great mercy he has given us new birth into a living hope through the resurrection of Jesus Christ from the dead, [4]and into an inheritance that can never perish, spoil or fade. This inheritance is kept in heaven for you, [5]who through faith are shielded by God's power until the coming of the salvation that is ready to be revealed in the last time. [6]In all this you greatly rejoice, though now for a little while you may have had to suffer grief in all kinds of trials. [7]These have come so that your faith—of greater worth than gold, which perishes even though refined by fire—may be proved genuine and may result in praise, glory and honor when Jesus Christ is revealed. [8]Though you have not seen him, you love him; and even though you do not see him now, you believe in him and are filled with an inexpressible and glorious joy, [9]for you are receiving the end result of your faith, the salvation of your souls.

THINK Peter starts off listing blessings stored up for us in heaven, indestructible benefits that are ours because we're children of God. But they're also things we start to enjoy today. So what all has God given us?

What is God's power doing for you right now?

Try this easier translation of 1 Peter 1:5: "And through your faith, God is protecting you by his power until you receive this salvation, which is ready to be revealed on the last day for all to see" (NLT). God will take care of you until he gives you the total fulfillment of your faith at the end of time.

Sounds great. But why is God letting his followers face trials?

LIVE How has God helped you when you've gone through tough times?

So why can you rejoice when trials hit?

The grammar of Peter's words in verse 6 means that—compared to the duration and greatness of heaven—the suffering we face now is brief and necessary. The apostle Paul said the same thing when he wrote that "what we suffer now is nothing compared to the glory he [God] will reveal to us later" (Romans 8:18, NLT).

Are these verses from Peter just happy words—or do they help you make sense of suffering? What do they do for you?

WRAP You won't escape trials. Yet God won't leave your side, making you tougher than any trouble you face and giving you a trust in him that's more valuable than gold.

» MORE THOUGHTS TO MULL

- Do you think Christians are fools to get hope from blessings God will give them in heaven?

- How has God used someone else's words to help you through suffering? What words haven't been helpful?

- Even if you're not facing something painful right now, someone you care about probably is. What can you do to help that person?

» MORE SCRIPTURES TO DIG

- The verses above come from the start of Peter's letter. Check out what he says near the end: "Give all your worries to him, because he cares about you" (**1 Peter 5:7**, NCV).

- Peter says that when fiery ordeals come to test us, we shouldn't be surprised "as though something strange were happening to you" (**1 Peter 4:12**). But he's careful to distinguish between the unavoidable pain we experience as followers of Jesus trying to do good and the misery we bring on ourselves because we do wrong (**1 Peter 3:13-17**).

- Flip to **James 1:2-4** for more encouragement in the middle of trials. The apostle James had the same goal as Peter—to give practical help to Christians who suffer as they follow God.

17. NO FEAR

1 Corinthians 15:55

"Where, O death, is your victory?
Where, O death, is your sting?"

START The Old Testament's idea of life after death was hazy. By the time the New Testament age arrived, some of God's people believed in a post-death resurrection, a belief they were willing to defend with fists (Acts 23:6-10). Jesus left no doubt: A time will come when the dead will hear his voice and pop from their graves (John 5:28-29). Being a Christian doesn't mean you'll never see the downside of death. But you can be certain there's something great to come.

How do you react to thoughts of your grand finale? Why? What do you expect death to be like?

READ 1 Corinthians 15:51-58

> [51]Listen, I tell you a mystery: We will not all sleep, but we will all be changed—[52]in a flash, in the twinkling of an eye, at the last trumpet. For the trumpet will sound, the dead will be raised imperishable, and we will be changed. [53]For the perishable must clothe itself with the imperishable, and the mortal with immortality. [54]When the perishable has been clothed with the imperishable, and the mortal with immortality, then the saying that is written will come true:
>
> "Death has been swallowed up in victory."
>
> [55]"Where, O death, is your victory?
>
> Where, O death, is your sting?"
>
> [56]The sting of death is sin, and the power of sin is the law. [57]But thanks be to God! He gives us the victory through our Lord Jesus Christ.
>
> [58]Therefore, my dear brothers and sisters, stand firm. Let nothing move you. Always give yourselves fully to the work of the Lord, because you know that your labor in the Lord is not in vain.

THINK What about us will change "in a flash"?

Our bodies are perishable, like bananas that will eventually go bad. When God changes us at the end of time, he will make our bodies imperishable— that is, immortal. That's tough to grasp when our eyes can only see birth, life, and death. But Paul's saying, "Look. What you know to be normal is going to totally change!"

What gives death its sting? What gives sin its power? What has Jesus done about sin and death?

Romans 6:23 says "The payment for sin is death. But God gives us the free gift of life forever in Christ Jesus our Lord" (NCV). The death of Jesus on the cross took care of the law's requirements (Romans 8:4). So by making forgiveness possible, Jesus destroys both sin and death.

Since these facts are true, how should we live? Why?

LIVE Do you really think you'll live after you die? Why—or why not?

This might be nice news for later, but you're probably not planning on dying anytime soon. What good does this information do you right now?

How do you think God wants you to feel about death?

WRAP Death is undeniably sad. Yet for Christians, sadness isn't the whole story. Paul wrote, "Brothers and sisters, we do not want you to be uninformed about those who sleep in death, so you do not grieve like the rest, *who have no hope*" (1 Thessalonians 4:13, italics added). When someone dies, you grieve. But you also believe in God's promise of eternal life (John 3:16).

» MORE THOUGHTS TO MULL

- Welsh poet Dylan Thomas penned these words to his critically ill father: "Do not go gentle into that good night, Old age should burn and rave at close of day; Rage, rage, against the dying of the light." When have you known someone who died without rage because he or she trusted God's promises about the life after death?

- If life is short and death is inevitable, why not squeeze in as much sin as you can?

- Sometimes life gets so sad you may wish you would die. If you or a friend feel that way, please tell an adult you trust.

» MORE SCRIPTURES TO DIG

- Eternal life isn't a make-believe promise to make you feel better when someone dies. Jesus' guarantee is clear: "I am the resurrection and the life. Anyone who believes in me will live, even after dying. Everyone who lives in me and believes in me will never ever die" (**John 11:25-26,** NLT). He said it again so you could be sure: "Because I live, you also will live" (**John 14:19**). And check out the promise he makes in **John 5:24.**

- The power that raised Christ will lift you from the grave (**1 Corinthians 6:14**). But God's resurrection power will also make you an unswerving follower of Jesus today. Like the apostle Paul wrote in a letter to his Ephesian friends, "I also pray that you will understand the incredible greatness of God's power for us who believe him. This is the same mighty power that raised Christ from the dead" (**Ephesians 1:19-20,** NLT). Ask God to fill you with that resurrection power right now.

18. REAL BELIEVERS

You can have authentic faith

James 2:14

What good is it, my brothers and sisters, if people claim to have faith but have no deeds? Can such faith save them?

START There's a classic evangelism pitch that starts, "God loves you and has a wonderful plan for your life." That promise is true for you and anyone willing to receive it. There's not an ounce of doubt that the Lord who came to give you life (John 10:10) wants you to thrive. But the most astonishing point of God's plan for your life is that you flourish best when you give yourself to others most. It's how you live out an authentic faith.

When have you found real life by doing good for someone other than yourself?

READ James 2:14-19

> [14]What good is it, my brothers and sisters, if people claim to have faith but have no deeds? Can such faith save them? [15]Suppose a brother or sister is without clothes and daily food. [16]If one of you says to them, "Go in peace; keep warm and well fed," but does nothing about their physical needs, what good is it? [17]In the same way, faith by itself, if it is not accompanied by action, is dead.
>
> [18]But someone will say, "You have faith; I have deeds."
>
> Show me your faith without deeds, and I will show you my faith by what I do. [19]You believe that there is one God. Good! Even the demons believe that—and shudder.

THINK There's no excuse for anyone in this scene not spotting the dire need. The person is literally naked—and hungry. He or she is within arm's reach, a member of the Christian community. What's wrong with the believer who walks by without doing something concrete to remedy the situation?

What good is our faith if it doesn't impact how we treat people?

How can you tell if someone has genuine faith?

There's nothing human beings can do to earn right standing with God (Romans 3:27-28). God gives salvation as a free gift to those who believe in Jesus (Romans 1:16). Yet the faith that makes us right with God produces good works. Our good actions don't save us, but they prove our faith is genuine, like fruit shows that a tree is alive and well. Our actions demonstrate what we truly believe and make our faith "complete" (James 2:22)—that is, "mature" or "perfect."

How is it possible for someone to believe in God yet not have real faith? Explain.

LIVE When have your actions as a Christian not lived up to your words?

Jesus once said, "Whoever wants to save their life will lose it, but whoever loses their life for me will find it" (Matthew 16:25). What gets in the way of giving up your life?

If you aim to experience the most fun and fulfilling life ever, how can you get that?

WRAP Thriving isn't just about developing your own life. It's watching out for the welfare of everyone.

» MORE THOUGHTS TO MULL

- If life works best when you look out for others, when is it right to worry about your own wants and needs?

- Are there times it's not good to give to others? Explain.

- Why is caring only for ourselves ultimately unfulfilling?

» MORE SCRIPTURES TO DIG

- In this passage James pictures a scene where a believer overlooks the desperate plight of a fellow Christian. God wants us to do good to all people, and we're doubly slack if we ignore the needs of spiritual family members. As the apostle Paul puts it, "Let us not become weary in doing good, for at the proper time we will reap a harvest if we do not give up. Therefore, as we have opportunity, let us do good to all people, especially to those who belong to the family of believers" (**Galatians 6:9-10**).

- Look to James for more practical wisdom on putting faith into action. He explains, for example, how words can be inflamed by hell itself and set all of life ablaze (**James 3:1-12**). He scolds those who play favorites, showing kindness to wealthy folks while disrespecting the poor (**James 2:1-11**). And he says real faith includes not just staying pure but taking care of the world's truly needy (**James 1:27**).

19. THE FLYING WALLENDAS

You'll get to God's goal

Philippians 1:6

Being confident of this, that he who began a good work in you will carry it on to completion until the day of Christ Jesus.

START Karl Wallenda of the Flying Wallendas was in his seventies when he plunged more than a hundred feet to his death while walking a tightwire between two office towers—a tragic fall after decades as the world's premier tightwire walker. After the accident Wallenda's wife reportedly said the stunt was the first time she'd ever seen her husband concerned about falling. Karl Wallenda fell, one observer concluded, because he focused on not falling—rather than on getting to the other side.

When have you feared you would fail to reach a goal? What worried you most?

READ Philippians 1:3-11

> ³I thank my God every time I remember you. ⁴In all my prayers for all of you, I always pray with joy ⁵because of your partnership in the gospel from the first day until now, ⁶being confident of this, that he who began a good work in you will carry it on to completion until the day of Christ Jesus.
>
> ⁷It is right for me to feel this way about all of you, since I have you in my heart and, whether I am in chains or defending and confirming the gospel, all of you share in God's grace with me. ⁸God can testify how I long for all of you with the affection of Christ Jesus.
>
> ⁹And this is my prayer: that your love may abound more and more in knowledge and depth of insight, ¹⁰so that you may be able to discern what is best and may be pure and blameless for the day of Christ, ¹¹filled with the fruit of righteousness that comes through Jesus Christ—to the glory and praise of God.

THINK God is going to finish his "good work" in the Philippians—and in us. What does that mean?

How long will God keep at this job?

The "day of Jesus Christ" is his return—that time when we'll be changed "in the twinkling of an eye" (1 Corinthians 15:52).

What major changes does Paul invite God to accomplish in his people? Finish up his prayers:

He wants them to have love that abounds in...

And knowledge that helps them...

So they can be...

And be filled with...

LIVE When you think about letting God rule in every part of your life, what feels hardest—so tough you shake with fear you won't be able to do it?

If God is doing all this work in you, why not just sit around, waiting for him to grow you?

How do you expect God to help you change? What practical steps can you take to let him work in you?

WRAP Your heart might be full of kakorrhaphiophobia—fear of failure. But the God who wants you to thrive guarantees to get you to his goals.

» MORE THOUGHTS TO MULL

- How was Paul's optimism about the Philippians rooted in reality? How had he already seen God at work in them?

- How would you like your relationship with God to grow in the next year?

- Pick out a friend who wants to thrive and grow close to God. Pray Paul's prayer for each other.

» MORE SCRIPTURES TO DIG

- God supplies every resource you need to grow. But he expects you to go for the goal. Later in this letter Paul says, "I press on to take hold of that for which Christ Jesus took hold of me...Forgetting what is behind and straining toward what is ahead, I press on toward the goal to win the prize for which God has called me heavenward in Christ Jesus" (**Philippians 3:12-14**).

- The "day of Jesus Christ" is the time in the future when Jesus will return to earth. It's when evildoers will be judged. But it's also when Christians will meet Jesus face-to-face and be fully changed so they are like him. Learn more about this in **1 Corinthians 1:8** and **5:5** as well as in **1 Thessalonians 5:2**.

- When Paul was imprisoned for his faith at Rome, the Christians at Philippi had sent money (**Philippians 1:5; 4:10-19**). Unlike others who were embarrassed when Paul was arrested, the Philippians stood rock-solid with him. Like him, they faced challenges from people who opposed their faith (**Philippians 1:29-30**). The Philippians had become some of the apostle Paul's closest friends.

20. YOUR DESTINY

You'll live with God and his people forever

Revelation 21:3

"Look! God's dwelling place is now among the people, and he will dwell with them. They will be his people, and God himself will be with them and be their God."

START If you want to get a glimpse of your eternal destiny, you have to flip to quite a few places in the Bible. Check out what's happening in heaven: Everyone does God's will (Matthew 6:10). God perfects our bodies (2 Corinthians 5:1-5) and transforms our whole selves (1 John 3:2). The worship rocks (Revelation 4). The Bible really does picture harps being strummed, although not everyone gets one (Revelation 5:8; 14:2; 15:2). It's a stunning place, portrayed with streets of gold and stacks of emeralds, amethyst, and pearls (Revelation 21:9-27). Human authors struggle to capture the greatness of heaven in words, but one point comes through clearly: It's thriving gone ultimate.

What do you think your future holds? And what does heaven have to do with it?

READ Revelation 21:1-7

¹ Then I saw "a new heaven and a new earth," for the first heaven and the first earth had passed away, and there was no longer any sea. ²I saw the Holy City, the new Jerusalem, coming down out of heaven from God, prepared as a bride beautifully dressed for her husband. ³And I heard a loud voice from the throne saying, "Look! God's dwelling place is now among the people, and he will dwell with them. They will be his people, and God himself will be with them and be their God. ⁴He will wipe every tear from their eyes. There will be no more death or mourning or crying or pain, for the old order of things has passed away."

⁵He who was seated on the throne said, "I am making everything new!" Then he said, "Write this down, for these words are trustworthy and true."

⁶He said to me: "It is done. I am the Alpha and the Omega, the Beginning and the End. To the thirsty I will give water without cost

from the spring of the water of life. [7]Those who are victorious will inherit all this, and I will be their God and they will be my children.

THINK What drops out of the sky at the start of this passage? Where did the old stuff go?

The word for "new" doesn't mean "second" but rather "transformed." So whatever you enjoy of God's creation—music, nature, color, beauty—will be present in abundance, with mindboggling intensity. God will no doubt create some amazing surprises, because our expectations are limited and warped (1 Corinthians 2:9). "No sea" means God has gotten rid of chaos. The "Holy City" is a place, but "bride" suggests it's also a group of people—God's people, as dazzling as a bride on her wedding day.

Who is at the center of heaven? What bad stuff has vanished?

God is the real life of this eternal party. He'll live close to us the way he's wanted to since he created this world—with no doubt, fear, or sin separating us from him. We'll know him as well as he knows us. And we'll celebrate him for giving us an eternity of friendship with himself and his people.

Who gets to enjoy all this great stuff—and God himself—forever?

Just like he does throughout the Bible, God issues an open invitation to all in Revelation 22:17: "Let those who are thirsty come; and let all who wish take the free gift of the water of life."

LIVE What painful things do you look forward to God wiping away in heaven?

What do you think of the destiny God has planned for you—life forever with him and his people in heaven?

WRAP Heaven is your real home. Yet almost everything you get in heaven you can start enjoying now—the transformed life God has planned for you. Grabbing hold of heaven is what thriving is all about.

» MORE THOUGHTS TO MULL

- So what do you think heaven is really like?

- What can you do right now to bring a slice of heaven to your life on earth?

- How do you want to keep thriving more and more now that you've wrapped up this book?

» MORE SCRIPTURES TO DIG

- As Jesus paid for the world's sins and breathed his last on the cross he cried out, "It is finished!" (**John 19:30**). Now in **Revelation 21:6** God proclaims that his plan is finally complete. He's the "Alpha and Omega" (the first and last letters of the Greek alphabet) and the "Beginning and the End." He's the being who began it all and controls all of history.

- Revelation shows people reaping the results of their all-important choice for or against God. Their wandering far from God becomes permanent, and they're sealed in a place apart from God's presence (**Revelation 21:8**).

- The apostle Paul says that if our Christian faith doesn't provide us with benefits beyond this life, we're pitiful (**1 Corinthians 15:19**). He asserts that we've believed in a worthless religion.

- All through the Bible you can spot God preparing a people to live with him: Check out **Genesis 17:7, Exodus 6:7, Leviticus 26:12, Jeremiah 31:33, Ezekiel 11:20, 2 Corinthians 6:16, Hebrews 8:10**, and **1 Peter 2:9-10**. And Jesus said heaven is all about knowing God: "This is eternal life: that they may know you, the only true God, and Jesus Christ, whom you have sent" (**John 17:3**).

In the Higher series, you'll find deep, interactive studies to help high school students engage with the Bible and develop a passionate, life-altering relationship with God. Each book has 20 studies, focusing on discipleship topics that are most relevant to high schoolers, and gets students to explore and study God's Word. In a voice that doesn't speak down to students, you'll find that these studies draw teens in and take them deeper into their faith.

Follow
Walk in the Rhythm of Jesus
978-0-310-28264-8

Soar
Fly into God's Plan for Your Future
978-0-310-28267-9

Think
Figure Out What You Believe and Why
978-0-310-28266-2

Thrive
Dare to Live Like God
978-0-310-28265-5

Kevin Johnson
Retail $8.99 each

Visit www.youthspecialties.com
or your local bookstore.

youth
specialties

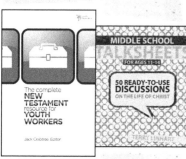

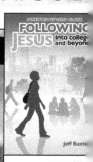

www.ingramcontent.com/pod-product-compliance
Ingram Content Group UK Ltd.
Pitfield, Milton Keynes, MK11 3LW, UK
UKHW031127120325
456135UK00006B/69